Bilingual: English — Japanese
バイリガル: 英語 — 日本語

Written by Tali Carmi
作:タリ・カーミ
Illustrated by Mindy Liang
絵:ミンディ・リアン
Translated by Sarah Ikeya
訳:いけや咲良

Terry Treetop and the Christmas Star
テリー・ツリートップと　クリスマス・スター
Tali Carmi
タリ・カーミ

Copyright © 2022 by Tali Carmi

All rights reserved. No part of this book may be used or reproduced in any manner whatsoever without the written and signed permission of the author, except in the case of brief quotations embodied in critical articles or review.

本書の著作権は著者に帰属します。
論評記事や評論における簡単な引用を除いて、文書による著者の許可なく、本書の一部あるいは全部をいかなる手段においても、複製、転載等することを禁じます。

Translated from the English by Sarah Ikeya
Illustrations by Mindy Liang

ISBN: 9789655752885

Here are some of the ways to contact me:
Mail: agency@ebook-pro.com
Instagram: tali.carmi
Website: www.thekidsbooks.com
Facebook: Tali.Carmi.Author
LinkedIn: Tali Carmi
Twitter: tbcarmi
Adress: Kaufmann St 2, Tel Aviv-Yafo, 6801294 Israel
Phone: +972-52-2237216

Terry Treetop
テリー・ツリートップと
and the Christmas Star
クリスマス・スター

Written by Tali Carmi

作: タリ・カーミ

It was Christmas Eve and the air smelled of cake,
People were skating on a big, frozen lake.
In windows, green and red lights were twinkling,
And all around you could hear small bells tinkling.

クリスマス・イブです。 あたり　いちめん　ケーキの　かおりが　ただよい
ひとびとは　おおきな　こおった　みずうみの　うえで　スケートを　しています。
まどべでは　みどりと　あかの　あかりが　キラキラと　かがやき
いたるところで　ちいさな　ベルの　チリンチリンと　なる　おとが　きこえます。

Mom was baking cookies, with flour in her hair,
Dad was hanging a garland around the door by the stairs.
Terry sat by the window with cocoa in his hand
Looking outside at the snow-covered land.

ママは かみの け に こむぎこが ついたままで クッキーを やいています。
パパは かいだんの そばの ドアの まわりに ガーランドを つるしています。
テリーは ココアを て に もったまま まどの そばに こしを おろし
ゆきに おおわれた そとの せかいを ながめています。

Outside, it had started heavily snowing
While in the hearth a warm fire was glowing.
The china laid out was the very best
Since they were expecting some wonderful guests.

そとでは　ゆきが　はげしく　ふりだしましたが
だんろでは　あたたかい　まっかな　ひ　が　かがやいています。
ならべられた　せとものは　とびきりの　じょうとうひん
なぜなら　これから　すばらしい　おきゃくさんたちが　くるからです。

Then Mom gave out a cry of panic so strong
That Terry and Dad turned to see what was wrong.
"I came out of the kitchen and what do I see?
We have not decorated our beautiful tree!"

と そのとき ママが パニックじょうたいで あまりに おおきな こえを あげたため
テリーと パパは どうしたのか たしかめようと ふりかえりました。
「ママが キッチンから でてきたら なにが みえたと おもう?
まだ きれいな ツリーの かざりつけを してなかったわ!」

"The guests are meant to arrive in an hour
And I am still all covered in flour!"
To their feet Terry and Dad quickly hopped,
Hanging the ornaments, from bottom to top.

「おきゃくさんたちは　1じかんごに　とうちゃく　よてい　なのに
ママは　まだ　こむぎこ　だらけよ!」
テリーと　パパは　いそいで　サッと　たちあがると
したから　うえまで　オーナメントを　つるしていきました。

All that was left was a bright, yellow star
When Dad said: "No, the top is too far.
I cannot reach it, I tried and I tried,
I'll have to get a ladder from the tree house outside."

あとは　ひかりかがやく　きいろの　スターだけ
と　そのとき　パパが　いいました。「ダメだ　てっぺんは　とおすぎる。
パパには　とどかない。　なんども　なんども　やってみたけど。
そとの　ツリーハウスから　ハシゴを　とってこなきゃ」

Terry took his binoculars from the small shelf
To check if Dad can carry the ladder by himself.
He pointed it at the snow-covered tree
And in it, he surely had something to see!

テリーは　パパが　ひとりで　ハシゴを　はこべるか　たしかめる　ために
ちいさな　たなから　そうがんきょうを　とりだしました。
そうがんきょうを　ゆきに　おおわれた　き　の　ほうに　むけると
き　の　なかには　たしかに　なにかが　いるのが　みえました！

He took his coat and followed his Dad through the snow
Which was up to his knees, so he was quite slow.
Terry yelled after him "Dad, can you see?
There's a frozen squirrel up in the tree!"

テリーは　コートを　とりだし　ゆきの　なか　パパを　おいかけました。
ヒザまで　つもった　ゆきの　せいで　ペースは　かなり　ゆっくりでした。
テリーは　パパの　うしろから　さけびました。「パパには　みえる？
き　の　うえで　リスが　1ぴき　こごえているんだ！」

Dad rushed to help but the tree was too tall,
And he saw that the ladder was no good at all.
It started to creak just under his toe,
A small crack - and his foot was back in the snow.

パパは　たすけようと　かけつけましたが　き　は　たかすぎるし
ハシゴも　まったく　やくに　たたないことが　わかりました。
ハシゴは　ちょうど　パパの　つまさきの　ましたで　キーキーと　きしみだし
ちいさな　ヒビが　―　そして　パパの　かたあしは　ゆきの　なかへ　ぎゃくもどり。

"It's dangerous to climb, now what will we do?"
Terry could see his Dad was worried too.
"Do not worry, Daddy, I will climb the tree,
It's not for nothing that Terry Treetop they call me!"

「のぼるのは　あぶないな。　さて　どうしようか?」
テリーには　パパも　しんぱいしているのが　わかりました。
「しんぱい　いらないよ　パパ。ぼくが　き　に　のぼるよから。
だてに　テリー・ツリートップと　よばれている　わけじゃない!」

Terry climbed to the treehouse, swift and fast-paced,
Knowing deep down that they had no time to waste.
Taking the squirrel, he climbed down with alarm,
Scared he might cause the poor creature some harm.

テリーは　またたくまに　きゅうピッチで　ツリーハウスへ　のぼりました。
こころの　おくそこで　むだに　している　じかんは　ないと　わかっていたのです。
テリーは　リスを　つかまえると　ビクビクしながら　おりていきました。
この　かわいそうな　いきものを　ケガさせてしまうかも　と　おそれながら。

They took it inside and wrapped it all snug,
In front of the fire, they laid it on the rug.
They put a hot water bottle right by its side
Everything they could think of that might help, they tried.

テリーと　パパは　リスを　いえの　なかへ　いれて　あたたかく　くるみ
ひ　の　まえの　ラグの　うえに　ねかせました。
ふたりは　リスの　すぐ　よこに　ゆたんぽを　おいて
たすけに　なるかも　しれないと　おもったことを　すべて　ためしました。

They were very worried for a creature that size
But soon it slowly opened its big, black eyes.
They gave it some water, it wiggled its nose,
And in a moment or two, to its feet it rose.

テリーと パパは あれほど ちいさな いきものの ことを とても しんぱいしましたが
ほどなくして リスは おおきな くろい め を ゆっくりと あけました。
ふたりが みずを あげると リスは はなを ピクピク うごかし
それから ちょっとして たちあがりました。

"What happened?" Terry asked, "Are you okay?"
The squirrel took a big breath and began to say:
"My name is Sammy and it's my first winter,
And I have never been much of a sprinter."

「なにが あったの?」 テリーは たずねました。「だいじょうぶ?」
リスは しんこきゅうを して はなしだしました。
「ぼくの なまえは サミー。 はじめての ふゆだし
しかも ぼくは たんきょりそうが あんまり とくいじゃないんだ」

"When it got cold, to their dens squirrels ran,
But I did not make any sort of plan.
Your treehouse looked like a good place to hide,
I thought it would be a bit warmer inside."

「さむくなって　ほかの　リスたちは　す　に　はしったけど
　ぼくには　とくに　これという　プランが　なかった。
　きみの　ツリーハウスは　かくれがに　よさそうだったし
　なかは　もうすこし　あたたかいだろうと　おもったんだ」

Then the doorbell rang and Terry made a plea:
"Sammy, will you please help us with our tree?"
With the star in this teeth, Sammy started to hop
And in a few seconds scurried straight to the top.

そのとき　よびりんが　なり　テリーは　ひっしになって　たのみました。
「サミー　おねがいだから　ツリーの　かざりつけを　てつだって　くれないかい?」
サミーは　スターを　くちに　くわえると　ピョンピョンと　とびはじめ
すうびょうごには　てっぺんまで　まっすぐ　チョコチョコと　はしっていきました。

The star shone brightly from the top of the tree,
Overlooking the guests, all happy to see
Terry's new friend Sammy among the twigs,
Enjoying his dinner – his favorite – dried figs!

ツリーの　てっぺんで　あかるく　かがやく　スターの　もとには
おきゃくさんたちが　みえます。　みんな　うれしそうです。
テリーの　あたらしい　おともだちの　サミーは　こえだの　あいだで
だいすきな　ほしイチジクの　ディナーを　たのしんでいます！

Thank You!

Thank you for purchasing this book!

You are welcome to visit my website,

play free educational online games and download free gifts.

この本をご購入くださり誠にありがとうございます！

私のサイトで無料のオンライン教育ゲームやギフトをお楽しみくださいませ。

Enjoy!

www.thekidsbooks.com

www.ingramcontent.com/pod-product-compliance
Lightning Source LLC
LaVergne TN
LVHW070427090526
838199LV00129B/477